Tony Hawk:
Skateboarding Legend

by Jeff Savage

Capstone
press

Mankato, Minnesota

Edge Books are published by Capstone Press
151 Good Counsel Drive, P.O. Box 669, Mankato, Minnesota 56002
www.capstonepress.com

Library of Congress Cataloging-in-Publication Data
Savage, Jeff, 1961–
    Tony Hawk : skateboarding legend / by Jeff Savage.
    p. cm.—(Edge books. Skateboarding)
    Includes bibliographical references and index.
    ISBN 0-7368-2704-8
    1. Hawk, Tony—Juvenile literature. 2. Skateboarders—United States—
Biography—Juvenile literature. I. Title. II. Series.
GV859.813.H39S38 2005
796.22'092—dc22   2004000658

Summary: Describes the life of skateboarder Tony Hawk, including early years,
    awards, and family life.

Editorial Credits
James Anderson, editor; Timothy Halldin, series designer; Enoch Peterson, book
    designer; Jo Miller, photo researcher; Eric Kudalis, product planning editor

Photo Credits
AP/Wide World Photos/Richard Drew, 26
Corbis/Duomo, 7, 28; NewSport/Rick Rickman, cover, 8; NewSport/X Games IX/
    Matt A. Brown, 4; Tim Rue, 18
Getty Images/Kevin Winter, 24
Glen E. Friedman, 10
Mercury Press/Isaac Hernandez, 23
Sports Illustrated/Richard Mackson, 16; V.J. Lovero, 15
Zuma Press/Shelly Castellano, 21

**Edge Books thanks Tod Swank, member, Board of Directors, International
Association of Skateboard Companies, for his assistance in preparing this book.**

The author dedicates this book to his son Taylor, who shares
Tony Hawk's birthday and his daredevil spirit.

Table of Contents

Tony Hawk first landed a 900 at the 1999 X Games.

The Birdman Soars

Tony Hawk stood tall on his skateboard atop a halfpipe. He looked down from the U-shaped ramp. Many people in the crowd at the 2003 Summer X Games chanted his name. They knew Tony was trying the ultimate trick. He wanted to land the 900.

Tony had landed the 900 at the 1999 and 2001 X Games, but never during his contest time. This time, when he spun two and one-half circles in the air, he wanted it to count.

Learn About

- The 900
- X Games medals
- The Tony Hawk Foundation

Tony had tried the 900 three times during the vert best trick event. On his fourth try, Tony dropped in on the slick wall of the ramp. He crouched low and glided across the ramp's transition. He flew off the ramp high into the air.

Tony was upside down as he went into a spin. He was nearly 20 feet (6 meters) above the ramp when he started to drop. He came down in a blur. His board hit the ramp safely. Tony had landed the 900.

The crowed screamed and cheered. Fans held signs with Tony's name on them. Some people held up their Tony Hawk skateboards. Tony took off his helmet and tossed it to the fans. He had just won his 16th medal at the X Games.

After the 2003 Summer X Games, Tony said he may not compete anymore. Instead, he may be an announcer for the X Games.

Tony's last X Games vert run may have been in 2003.

The Greatest Ever

Most people agree that Tony is the greatest skater ever. Through 2003, he entered 103 events and won 73 of them, including 16 medals at the X Games. He has invented more than 80 tricks.

Tony helps make skating popular. Video games, toys, and clothing companies use his name. His company, the Tony Hawk Foundation, gives money to help build skateparks around the country. Many people who don't know a lot about skating know Tony Hawk's name. Tony is a skateboarding legend.

Fans often ask Tony to sign autographs.

Tony skated at a young age.

CHAPTER TWO

Learning to Skate

From a very early age, Tony was serious about sports. On April 12, 1968, Anthony Frank Hawk was born in Carlsbad, California. Young Tony played baseball and basketball. His father, Frank, was Tony's Little League baseball coach.

Tony always wanted to do well in sports. Once, when Tony was 6, he struck out in a baseball game. He was so upset that he hid in a nearby ravine. Another time, Tony got angry because he couldn't hold his breath long enough to swim across a large pool.

Learn About

- Other sports
- Tony's first board
- The ollie

Tony Hawk's X Games Wins

2003

Gold - vert best trick

2002

Gold - vert doubles

Bronze - vert best trick

2001

Gold - vert doubles

Silver - vert best trick

2000

Gold - vert doubles

1999

Gold - vert best trick

Gold - vert doubles

Bronze - vert

1998

Gold - vert doubles

Bronze - vert

1997

Gold - vert

Gold - vert doubles

1996

Silver - vert

1995

Gold - vert

Gold - park

Big Brother's Board

Tony was 9 when his older brother Steve gave him an old skateboard. Steve taught Tony how to skate on sidewalks.

Soon, Tony practiced at skateparks around San Diego. Tony was skinny and tall for his age. He had a hard time getting the speed he needed to go up a ramp and get into the air. But he fixed his problem. He invented his own skating style.

Tony was better at skating than he was at other sports. Skating made Tony feel confident. Tony wanted to keep practicing and learning new tricks. Tony's parents had to beg him to come home from the skateparks.

Making Up His Mind

When Tony was 11, he was trying to learn a move called a frontside rock-and-roll. But he had to leave the skatepark and give up for the day. He was late for basketball practice. He raced to the gym still wearing his kneepads. He wished he were back at the skatepark.

That night, Tony made a decision. He told his parents that he didn't want to play other sports anymore. He just wanted to skate.

Tony soon entered contests. His style was still different from other skaters. He did not have the upper-body strength to grab his board in midair and pin it to his feet. So he became one of the first skaters to use a move called the ollie. He would spring into the air with the board on his feet, as if it were stuck there. By age 12, he won several local contests.

Sticking With It

At school, some kids teased Tony. They told him that skating was for losers. The teasing hurt Tony's feelings, but he continued to skate.

Tony became a great skater as a teenager.

Tony worked hard at the skateparks. He created new tricks like the backside varial and the ollie-to-indy. Tony was quiet and focused as he tried to learn the moves. In just a few years, Tony was a top-ranked skater worldwide.

Tony took part in contests while he was still in high school.

CHAPTER THREE

Creating Tricks

As a teenager, Tony made money doing what he loved. He earned some prize money from contests. But most of his money came from royalties and sponsorship deals. Companies used his name to sell their products. He traveled around the world showing skateboard products. At age 17, while in high school, Tony bought his own house. At 19, he was earning $200,000 a year. Still, Tony thought that skateboarding might lose popularity. He wasn't sure skateboarding could be a career.

Learn About

- Sponsorships
- Birdhouse Projects
- The Extreme Games

Birdhouse Projects sponsors skaters like Shaun White (right).

Businessman

Tony always kept an eye on the business side of the sport. When one of his sponsors started to lose money, Tony started a company called Birdhouse Projects. Birdhouse makes skateboards, skateboard parts, and clothes. Later, he started Hawk Clothing, which makes clothes for kids.

Tony didn't have much time for dating while he was on skateboard tours. When Tony's companies were successful, he had some time to settle down. He was soon married and had a son named Riley.

Twists and Turns

Tony's life took a turn as the skateboard business changed. Kids started riding bikes instead of skateboards. Many skateparks closed. Tony struggled to make his house payment each month. In 1995, Tony and his wife divorced.

Later in 1995, both Tony and skating made a comeback. The ESPN TV network held an action sports contest called the Extreme Games. The contest was later named the X Games. Tony won the first ever vert event and got second in the street event. Many people saw Tony on TV.

X Games Success

After the Extreme Games, Tony's life turned around again. In 1996, Tony married his second wife, Erin. They bought a large house with a pool and waterfall. Tony also built a halfpipe in his yard. He invented new tricks on his ramp. The cab-to-backside and the switch 540 became easy for Tony. People began to think of Tony as the king of skating.

Tony spends time skating with his son Riley.

At the 1997 X Games in San Diego, California, Tony showed his talent. On his final run, he landed all 17 of the tricks he tried. He landed four 540s in a row. Tony's run at that contest may be one of the greatest skating runs ever.

Two years later, at the 1999 Summer X Games, after his time ran out, Tony landed the first 900. After the move, Tony talked to reporters. He told them that he made a decision before the run. He was going to land the 900 or be carried off the ramp on a stretcher.

Tony landed the first 900 at the X Games in 1999.

Tony won an ESPN award in 2001.

Superstar

Tony has been to the hospital many times. He has suffered broken bones and broken teeth. His front teeth are false because he broke out his real teeth. Tony has been knocked unconscious more than 10 times.

Soaring Popularity

No matter how many injuries Tony suffered, he continued to skate. The tricks he invented improved skateboarding. In 2001, he received an ESPN Action Sports Achievement Award. He is known all over the world as a master of the sport. He has been on TV and in movies.

Learn About

- ⬭ **Injuries**
- ⬭ **Awards**
- ⬭ **Video games**

Tony is featured as a remote-controlled toy.

Mr. Skateboarding

Companies still hire Tony to advertise their products. Tony has worked with Mattel toys, Quicksilver clothing, and McDonald's restaurants. People buy Tony Hawk remote-controlled skateboards and Tony Hawk snack foods. Tony has done commercials for milk and milk shakes.

In 1999, a video game called Tony Hawk's Pro Skater was released. It quickly moved to the top of the sales charts. Millions of copies of the game have been sold. In 2003, a new game called Tony Hawk's Underground became popular. Tony once told a video game magazine that he rates himself between good and excellent at playing video games.

Trivia

The Boom Boom HuckJam is a tour of the best skaters, BMX riders, and motocross riders. Tony started the tour to let more people know about action sports.

Love of the Sport

Tony lives with his family in a $2 million home in California. When he can, he stays at home with his younger boys, Spencer and Keegan. He picks up Riley after school. Tony is in charge of the Tony Hawk Foundation, which has built about 100 skateparks around the country.

Some skaters think that Tony has made skating too commercial. They think the sport should remain out of the spotlight. But Tony has said that he does not want to be an actor or a salesman. He just wants to be known as a skater.

Tony earned $10 million in 2001, and more in 2002 and 2003. But Tony says he does not love skating for the money. He says it has been the way that he has expressed himself since he was 9 years old.

Tony still spends a lot of time on halfpipes.

Glossary

achievement (uh-CHEEV-muhnt)—to do something successfully

advertise (AD-ver-tize)—to give information about something that a company wants to sell

commercial (kuh-MUR-shuhl)—having money as the main goal

foundation (foun-DAY-shuhn)—a group that gives money to good causes

ravine (ruh-VEEN)—a deep, narrow valley with steep sides

royalties (ROI-uhl-tees)—money paid based on the number of items sold

sponsorship (SPON-sur-ship)—when companies pay a skater to use and advertise their products

transition (tran-ZISH-uhn)—the curved parts of a halfpipe

unconscious (uhn-KOHN-shuhss)—not awake, not able to see, feel, or think

Read More

Braun, Eric. *Tony Hawk*. Amazing Athletes. Minneapolis: Lerner, 2003.

Savage, Jeff. V*ert Skating: Mastering the Ramp*. Skateboarding. Mankato, Minn.: Edge Books, 2005.

Stout, Glenn. *On the Halfpipe with Tony Hawk*. Boston: Little Brown & Co., 2001.

Internet Sites

FactHound offers a safe, fun way to find Internet sites related to this book. All of the sites on FactHound have been researched by our staff.

Here's how:

1. Visit *www.facthound.com*
2. Type in this special code **0736827048** for age-appropriate sites. Or enter a search word related to this book for a more general search.
3. Click on the **Fetch It** button. FactHound will fetch the best sites for you!

Index